MODERN MEDICINE

Chris Oxlade

www.raintreepublishers.co.uk
Visit our website to find out
more information about
Raintree books.

To order:
☏ Phone 0845 6044371
📄 Fax +44 (0) 1865 312263
💻 Email myorders@raintreepublishers.co.uk

Customers from outside the UK please telephone +44 1865 312262

Raintree is an imprint of Capstone Global Library
Limited, a company incorporated in England and
Wales having its registered office at 7 Pilgrim Street,
London, EC4V 6LB – Registered company number:
6695582

Edited by Andrew Farrow, Adam Miller, and
  Vaarunika Dharmapala
Designed by Philippa Jenkins
Picture research by Ruth Blair
Originated by Capstone Global Library Ltd
Printed and bound in China by Leo Paper
  Products Ltd

ISBN 978 1 406 23874 7 (hardback)
16 15 14 13 12
10 9 8 7 6 5 4 3 2 1

British Library Cataloguing in Publication Data
Oxlade, Chris.
Modern medicine. -- (Medicine through the ages)
610.9'04-dc22
A full catalogue record for this book is available
from the British Library.

Acknowledgements
We would like to thank the following for permission
to reproduce photographs: Corbis pp. 5 (© Mika),
8 (© Salvatore Di Nolfi/EPA), 9 (© Louie Psihoyos),
15 (© Yang Liu), 16 (© Hugh Sitton), 17, 28, 33
(© Bettmann), 20, 24 (© Hulton-Deutsch Collection),
30 (© Najlah Feanny), 31 (© Mike F. Alquinto/
EPA), 32 (© John Stanmeyer/VII), 34 (© Stephen
Morrison/EPA), 35 (© Reuters), 36 (© Keren Su),
37 (© aman/Demotix), 40 (© Lucas Jackson/
Reuters); © Corbis pp. 26, 27; Getty Images pp.
12 (Hulton Archive), 23 (Per-Anders Pettersson),
29 (Marco Di Lauro), 41 (Science Photo Library/
Coneyl Jay); Science Photo Library pp. 6 (Zephyr),
7 (Gastrolab), 10 (Jan Halaska), 18 (James King-
Holmes), 22 (Andy Crump, TDR, WHO);
Shutterstock pp. 11 (© Fanfo), 39 (© Deklofenak);
Wellcome Library, London pp. 13, 14, 19, 25, 38.

Cover photograph of *Operation*, 1929 (oil on canvas)
by Christian Schad (1894–1982), reproduced with
permission of Bridgeman Art Library (© Christian
Schad Stiftung Aschaffenburg/VG Bild-Kunst, Bonn
and DACS, London 2011).

Every effort has been made to contact copyright
holders of any material reproduced in this book. Any
omissions will be rectified in subsequent printings if
notice is given to the publisher.

Disclaimer
All the internet addresses (URLs) given in this book
were valid at the time of going to press. However,
due to the dynamic nature of the internet, some
addresses may have changed, or sites may have
changed or ceased to exist since publication. While
the author and publisher regret any inconvenience
this may cause readers, no responsibility for any
such changes can be accepted by either the author
or the publisher.

Contents

Some words are shown in bold, **like this**. You can find out what they mean by looking in the glossary. You can also look out for them in the "Word Station" box at the bottom of each page.

A transformation in medicine

The 20th century was a time of extraordinary change, and no more so than in the world of medicine. For example, diseases that were killers in 1900, such as polio, were almost wiped out. Hundreds of new drugs were developed. Today's extraordinary surgical techniques, such as heart transplants, would have been unthinkable for a doctor 100 years ago. In 1900, very few people could have afforded to see that doctor. Today, in many countries people can see a doctor or other healthcare worker when they need to, often for free.

This diagram shows the main factors for change that led to improved medicine and health in the 20th century.

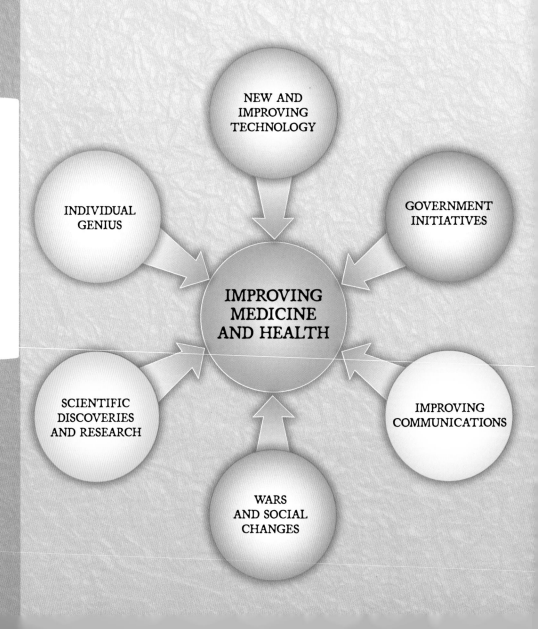

NEW AND IMPROVING TECHNOLOGY

GOVERNMENT INITIATIVES

INDIVIDUAL GENIUS

IMPROVING MEDICINE AND HEALTH

SCIENTIFIC DISCOVERIES AND RESEARCH

IMPROVING COMMUNICATIONS

WARS AND SOCIAL CHANGES

A new approach

At the beginning of the 20th century, doctors used many medical treatments because they thought they worked. There was, however, no real evidence that many of them did. During the 20th century, this changed. Modern drugs and other treatments are now only used after they have been tried out in tests called **clinical trials**. The results from a trial are evidence that the treatments work. This approach is called evidence-based medicine.

Evidence of change

There is plenty of evidence of the success of modern medicine and improvements in public health. Two of the most important pieces of evidence are **life expectancy** and infant mortality. Life expectancy is how long, on average, a person lives. Infant mortality is the number of babies that die before their first birthday, normally shown as deaths per thousand babies born.

Since 1900, life expectancy for men in the United States has increased from 46 years to 75 years. Infant mortality has dropped from 140 deaths per 1,000 births to just 6. Figures are similar for the United Kingdom. It is important to remember, however, that life expectancy and infant mortality have been improved by other factors, too. For example, rising living standards, better nutrition, and cultural changes have also played their part.

FACTORS FOR CHANGE

WHAT IS A FACTOR FOR CHANGE?

A factor for change is an event or idea that causes changes, in this case, in the world of medicine. For example, the two world wars of the 20th century changed many things about medicine and health. The diagram on page 4 shows other factors for change.

Increasing life expectancy means that, today, many people enjoy life into their 80s and 90s.

Technical advances

Today, doctors and nurses use many incredible technologies and surgical techniques. These allow doctors to **diagnose** and cure diseases, and treat injuries that would have killed people in the past. Faster surgery and less painful recovery for patients are also possible.

Scanners

Doctors have a range of machines for looking inside patients' bodies. The **ultrasound** scanner was developed in the 1940s. This sends high-pitched sound into the body and builds a picture by detecting echoes. Since the 1960s, the development of babies in their mothers' wombs has been checked with ultrasound. The 1970s saw the development of two new scanners that make highly detailed images of the body. The computed tomography (CT) scanner uses **X-rays** to build images. The MRI scanner uses super-strong magnets to make images. Generally, but not always, CT scanners are used to look at bony structures, and MRI scanners to look at soft tissues.

FACTORS FOR CHANGE

COMPUTER POWER

Medical technology such as CT scanners and MRI scanners would not be possible without computers. The development of computers, which began in the 1940s, was a vital factor for change in the world of modern medicine. Today, patient medical records (details of the treatments they have had in the past) can be kept on computer for quick reference.

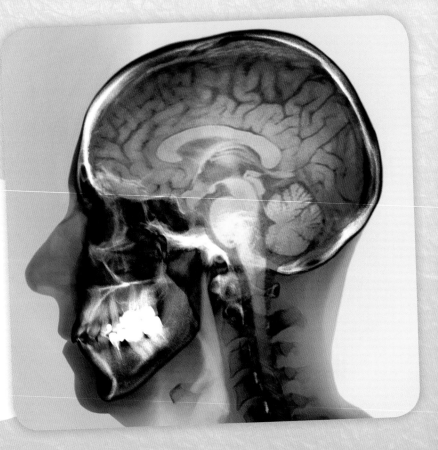

This MRI scan of a patient's brain shows tissues and any possible damage caused to them by disease.

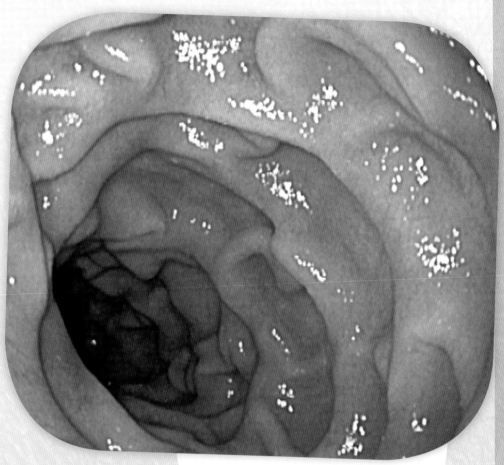

 This is a view through an endoscope into a patient's small intestine.

Endoscopes

An **endoscope** is a device that allows doctors to actually see inside a patient's body. It is a long, narrow tube inserted into the body through an opening, such as the mouth. Simple endoscopes were developed in the 19th century, but the images they produced were not very good.

A breakthrough came in the 1950s with the invention of the fibroscope by Harold Hopkins (see panel on the right). It used glass fibres both to illuminate inside the body and to bring images out.

HAROLD HOPKINS
(1918–1994)

Harold Hopkins was a British physicist who improved endoscopes in the 1950s and 1960s. Hopkins was born in Leicester and studied optics as a student. He worked with surgeons to improve the endoscope, and made it a far more useful tool for them. Hopkins also developed better lenses for television cameras.

WORD STATION
endoscope medical instrument that can be inserted into the body and allows doctors to see inside their patients

7

Keyhole surgery

In **keyhole surgery** (also called laparoscopic surgery), a surgeon inserts surgical instruments into the body through small holes (about a centimetre across) in the skin. The surgeon uses an endoscope (see page 7) to see what he or she is doing. Keyhole surgery became widely used in the 1990s. Before then, all operations involved making large incisions, often through layers of muscle, to reach the site of the operation. This meant more discomfort and longer recovery time for the patient. A more recent development is the use of robots in keyhole surgery. They can position instruments very precisely.

Microsurgery

In the 1960s, surgeons, including Harry Buncke (see panel on the left), developed a technique called **microsurgery**. This involves repairing tiny blood vessels and nerves. The surgeon uses a microscope to see what he or she is doing. Microsurgery is used mainly in plastic surgery (reshaping and repairing skin and bone). It even allows surgeons to re-attach fingers, arms, and feet that have been accidentally chopped off!

These surgeons are performing keyhole surgery using a robot. Each arm of the robot is holding an instrument.

HARRY BUNCKE
(1922–2008)

Harry Buncke was a US surgeon who became known as the "father of microsurgery". Often working in his own garage, Buncke designed and made tiny surgical needles himself, and used them to form tiny stitches. He performed his first microsurgery on a patient in 1969.

Did you know?
Buncke practised his stitching by re-attaching an ear to a rabbit.

WORD STATION
keyhole surgery surgery that is carried out through a very small cut in the body

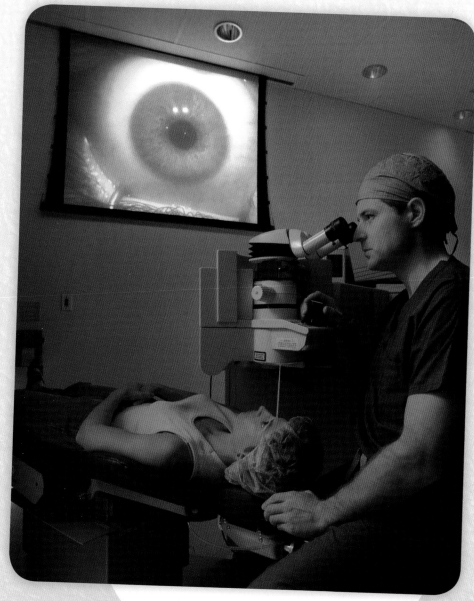

Today, laser eye surgery is
an everyday operation.

THE INVENTION OF LASERS

A laser emits a thin, powerful beam of light. The first laser was built in 1960. Within a few years, surgeons were using lasers in surgery. The laser is one of many examples of where new scientific discoveries and technologies have been applied to medicine.

Laser surgery

The laser scalpel was developed in the 1960s. Surgeons use laser scalpels to slice through tissue, and to remove damaged tissues by vaporizing them. Laser scalpels also reduce bleeding from cuts by sealing tiny blood vessels with their heat. The first laser eye surgery was performed in the 1990s. In eye surgery, a laser accurately shapes the **cornea** at the front of the eye to correct the patient's vision.

WORD STATION
cornea transparent layer at the front of a person's eye, which can become opaque (not able to be seen through) because of certain illnesses

Mending the heart

Until the middle of the 20th century, heart surgery was almost impossible. Surgeons could not stop the heart to work on it, because this would have killed the patient. In 1953, the first heart operation was performed with the aid of a heart-lung bypass machine, by US surgeon John Gibbon. This machine does the job of a patient's heart and lungs while the heart is stopped. Heart surgery now saves the lives of thousands of people.

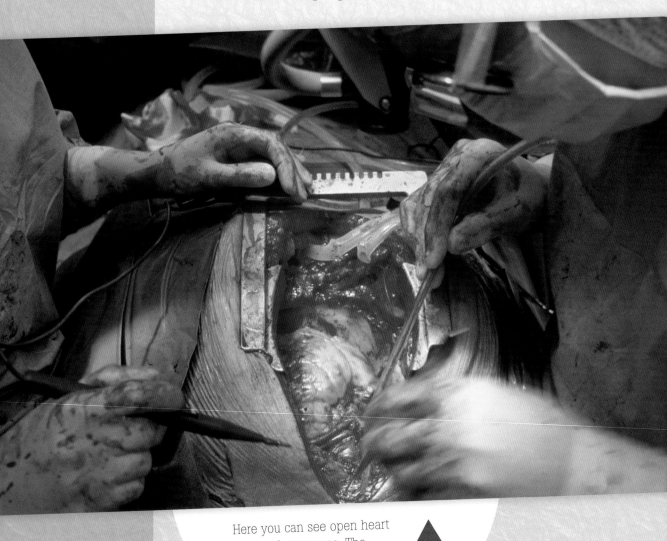

Here you can see open heart surgery in progress. The patient's ribcage has been opened to reveal the heart.

A machine called a defibrillator is used to restart a stopped heart, or a heart that is not beating properly. It uses a small electric shock to make the heart muscles beat properly. Portable defibrillators, used in hospital wards and ambulances, were developed in the 1960s.

Heart attacks are often caused by blockages in the blood vessels that supply blood to the heart. These are called the **coronary arteries**. In 1964, US surgeon Charles Dotter invented a way of opening up the blocked arteries, a procedure known as angioplasty. A thin wire (known as a catheter) with a tiny balloon on the end is pushed along the artery. The balloon is then inflated, which breaks the blockage.

Baby incubators

Babies are sometimes born many weeks before they should be, before their bodies are properly grown. These babies are called premature babies. Today, premature babies are looked after in a **neonatal** intensive care unit, or baby incubator. This machine keeps them warm and feeds them until they are fully developed babies. Even babies that weigh as little as 500 grams (17.6 ounces) can survive. The incubator has saved the lives of thousands of babies. It is one factor in the reduction in child mortality.

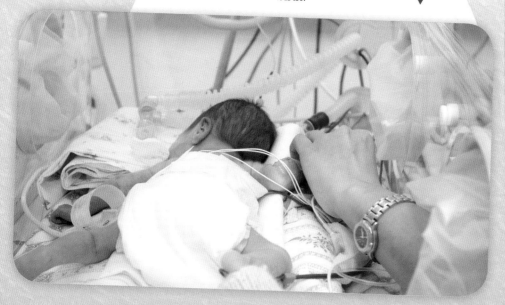

A hundred years ago, this premature baby would almost certainly have died soon after birth.

IMPROVING ANAESTHESIA

Early **anaesthetic** drugs, such as chloroform, had nasty side effects and sometimes caused death. In the early decades of the 20th century, better anaesthetic drugs and techniques were developed. These included drugs that were injected instead of inhaled. Anaesthetists now have a range of drugs that are safe for patients and have few side effects. They also use electronic systems to monitor patients while they are "under".

CHRISTIAAN BARNARD
(1922–2001)

Christiaan Barnard was a South African heart surgeon who performed the world's first heart transplant. As a student, Barnard walked 8 kilometres (5 miles) each day to study at college. In 1958, he became a heart surgeon at the University of Cape Town. Here, he thought about the possibility of heart transplants, before performing his famous operation.

"On Saturday, I was a surgeon in South Africa, very little known. On Monday, I was world renowned."

Christiaan Barnard

Transplant surgery

A transplant is an operation in which surgeons replace a diseased or damaged part of a body in one patient (the recipient) with a part from another person (the donor, who has normally died). Kidney, liver, pancreas, heart, lungs, and even hand and face transplants are possible today. Thousands of people live today who would have died before transplants were developed. Transplants became possible because of developments in surgery such as microsurgery. The first successful transplant – a kidney transplant – took place in 1954. Kidney transplants have saved hundreds of thousands of lives since.

The first heart transplant operation was performed by Christiaan Barnard in South Africa in 1967. The recipient, Louis Washkansky, survived the operation, but died 18 days later. The heart came from a young woman.

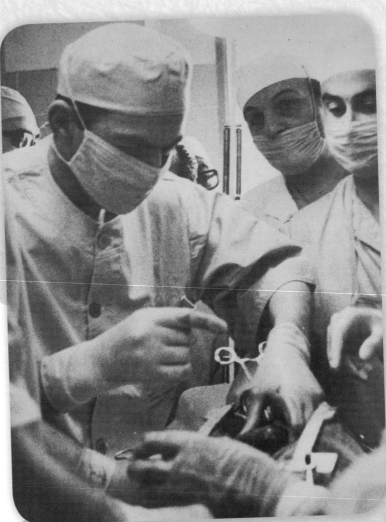

This is Christiaan Barnard practising his heart transplant surgery on a dog in 1968. This dog did not survive the operation.

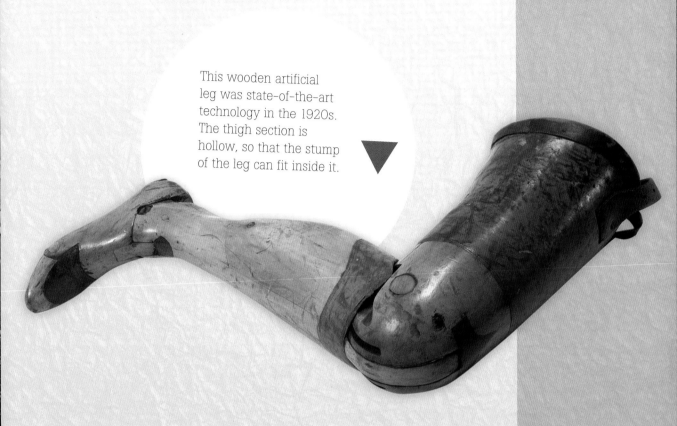

This wooden artificial leg was state-of-the-art technology in the 1920s. The thigh section is hollow, so that the stump of the leg can fit inside it.

A major problem with early transplants was rejection. This happened because a patient's **immune system** treats another person's organ like an infection and tries to destroy it. This problem has been overcome with special drugs. Surgeons gradually learned from both their successes and failures. By the 1980s, patients were surviving for many years with their replacement organs.

Artificial body parts

Some damaged or diseased body parts can be replaced by artificial parts. Simple artificial (or prosthetic) limbs, such as false legs, have been around for hundreds of years, but recent advances are dramatic. Artificial arms now have electronics that detect the user's nerve signals, so the user can grip and release objects with the fingers.

Artificial hearts are given to patients who are waiting for a heart transplant. In 1982, the first patient to receive an artificial heart was a US dentist called Barney Clark. Clark lived for 117 days, but had to be permanently attached to a power supply for the heart. Research continues into developing an artificial heart that can be installed permanently in a patient.

Fighting disease

Today, we can successfully fight hundreds of illnesses and diseases which were killers at the start of the 20th century. We can do this because, during the 20th century, scientists made many discoveries about how our bodies work. They also discovered how diseases spread and affect our bodies. These findings are the result of medical research. This knowledge has allowed other scientists to develop drugs and other treatments to fight disease.

Synthetic drugs

For hundreds of years, people have known that certain plants help to relieve the symptoms of disease, such as fever and headache. The plants contain chemicals that do the job. In the 19th century, scientists learned how to extract these natural chemicals. They used them to make drugs. In the 20th century, scientists learned how to create **synthetic** drugs, too. Early work on synthetic drugs was carried out by German scientist Paul Ehrlich. In 1910, he made the very first synthetic drug, called salvarsan. Ehrlich made salvarsan to treat a disease called **syphilis**. He experimented with hundreds of chemicals before discovering that salvarsan worked.

Hunt's Remedy claimed to cure "all diseases of the kidneys, bladder, liver, and urinary organs". Today, this boast would need evidence to back it up.

This large-scale factory is the modern face of drug production.

THALIDOMIDE

Thalidomide was a drug used as a sedative (to calm down patients). It was first given to patients in 1957. Many pregnant women took the drug. Sadly, thousands of babies whose mothers took thalidomide were born with physical disabilities. This was because the effects of the drug on developing babies were not tested before it was allowed on to the market. The drug company that developed thalidomide provided some help to the surviving sufferers.

Ehrlich also came up with the word *chemotherapy* for fighting disease with chemicals. Doctors now have a vast range of drugs to call on. They prescribe them for fighting diseases and infections, reducing pain, improving digestion, and numerous other jobs.

Developing a drug

By the 1950s, a huge drug-making industry, called the **pharmaceutical** industry, had grown up. Drugs companies design, test, manufacture, and then sell drugs for profit. Making a new drug for a certain job is a long process. Scientists create many different chemicals before deciding which ones to test. The drug is tested in a **clinical trial** to see if it has the desired effect. If it works, the drug must then be approved by the government before being sold.

Vaccines

A **vaccine** is a drug that stops a person catching a disease. For example, giving a person a measles vaccine makes sure that the person never catches measles. We say it makes them immune from the disease. A vaccine contains a weakened or dead version of the bacteria or **virus** that causes the disease.

Vaccines have been developed for many killer diseases, such as cholera and influenza (flu). Through the use of vaccines, some areas of the world are free of some diseases. An example is polio, which attacks the nervous system. The first polio vaccine was developed by Jonas Salk (see panel on the left) and came into use in 1955. Four years later, the number of cases of polio in the United States had fallen by 90 per cent. Since then, there has been a worldwide vaccination programme against polio. Today, there are just a few thousand cases a year.

This baby is being given a vaccine by mouth in order to prevent diseases in later life.

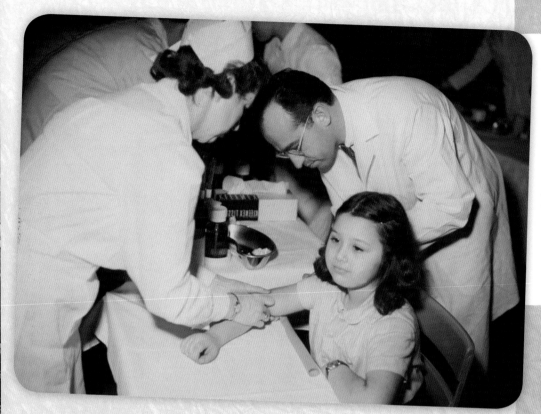

Here, Jonas Salk and a nurse administer a polio vaccination to a young girl.

The fight against cancer

Cancer happens when cells in the body start growing out of control. In developed countries, one in three people suffer from cancer at some point in their lives. Since the middle of the 20th century, there have been many advances in **diagnosing** and treating disease (including surgery, radiation therapy, and chemotherapy). Today, although we cannot prevent cancer, people who suffer from it have a much better chance of survival. We also know that the chances of getting certain cancers can be reduced by not smoking and eating a healthy diet.

Mental health

Illnesses that change how people behave are called mental illnesses. Ways of treating mental disease have changed greatly over the last 100 years. In the 1930s, doctors tried electric shock treatment. In the 1940s, they tried a type of brain surgery called lobotomy. In a lobotomy, nerve links in the brain were cut to try to cure certain mental illnesses. Mental patients were sometimes locked away in mental hospitals. From the 1950s, doctors turned to drugs, such as antidepressants, to treat mental illness. We now understand these diseases better, and patients are treated with modern drugs and **psychotherapy**. Even so, mental illness is still not fully understood.

Inheriting disease?

People often think that if a disease has affected their parents and grandparents, then they are likely to inherit the disease. This is true for some diseases, such as Huntington's disease. For most diseases, however, it is a minor factor. It might make it a little more likely that the person will get a disease, but poor diet and lifestyle, and lack of exercise can be much more important factors.

Understanding DNA

DNA is a chemical that is found in every cell in your body. DNA is short for deoxyribonucleic acid. It is an amazingly complicated chemical. It contains a chemical code that controls how a body grows, how it works, and how it fights disease. DNA is passed from parents to children, which is why you have similar characteristics to your parents.

Some diseases are caused by faults in DNA. They include **cystic fibrosis** and **sickle-cell disease**. These diseases can be passed from parents to their children, and are known as hereditary diseases. The fact that DNA is responsible for hereditary diseases was discovered in 1943. Another important discovery was the structure of DNA, made by Francis Crick and James Watson in 1953.

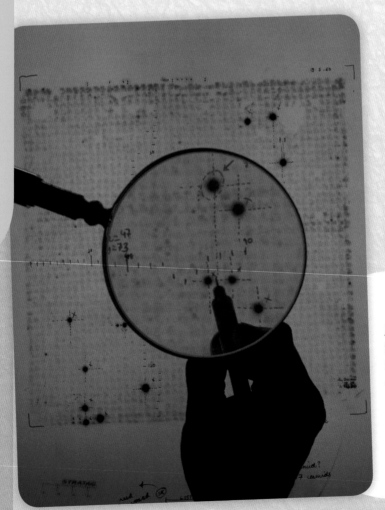

A researcher is examining fragments of DNA during research into inherited breast cancer.

WORD STATION
cystic fibrosis disease that is inherited by children from their parents. It can cause the lungs to become clogged with thick mucus.

Sickle-cell disease is an inherited disease that affects the shape of the blood cells.

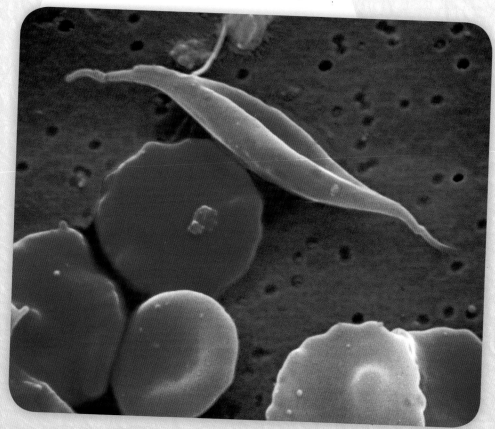

THE HUMAN GENOME PROJECT

The human genome is all the genetic information contained in a human cell. It is made up of around 25,000 genes. In 1990, scientists of the Human Genome Project began working out the information in each gene. The complex project was completed in 2003. The project allowed scientists to identify which genes caused certain diseases.

Genes and genetics

A **gene** is a piece of information that is coded in DNA. Different genes control how different parts of your body grow and how they work (for example, one gene controls your hair colour, another gene controls your blood group). Genetics is the branch of science that studies genes. Because some genes are responsible for fighting disease, and faulty genes can cause disease, genetics is vital in modern medicine. Doctors can now predict if children are likely to suffer from different hereditary diseases in later life.

Public health

Public health is all about keeping the population of a country healthy. It means making sure people have access to medical care when they are ill. It also means making sure people have healthy homes and are educated about leading a healthy lifestyle (eating healthy food and doing exercise). In the last century, public health has improved massively.

Housing

In 1900, hundreds of thousands of people lived in overcrowded slums in towns and cities. Whole families were crammed into tiny houses with no fresh water supply and no toilets. These conditions allowed diseases such as typhoid, cholera, and tuberculosis to spread easily. The situation slowly improved through the first half of the 20th century. In the major cities in Europe and North America, many slums were demolished and replaced by new, more spacious housing.

This is Londonderry, Northern Ireland in 1955. At that time, many people were still living in unhealthy slum housing.

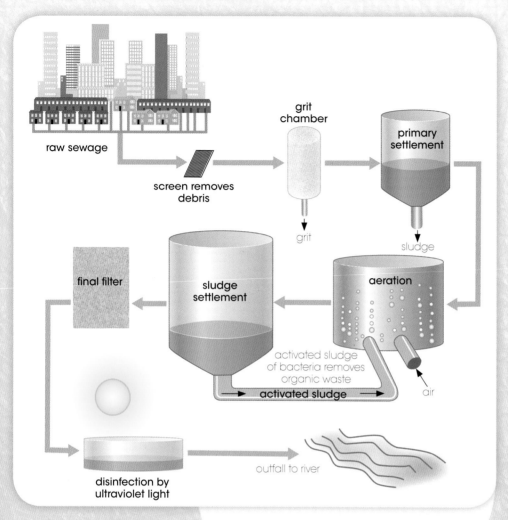

grit
chamber

primary
settlement

raw sewage

screen removes
debris

grit

sludge

final filter

sludge
settlement

aeration

activated sludge
of bacteria removes
organic waste

activated sludge

air

disinfection by
ultraviolet light

outfall to river

These are the processes that clean sewage at water treatment plants.

Water supplies and sanitation

You do not need a medical expert to tell you that water is vital for your health. You have to drink water, and wash with water. For you to stay healthy, the water must be clean. Drinking dirty water is a major cause of disease around the world. In the old city slums, lack of **sanitation** meant that local water sources became dirty with human waste. As new houses were built, they were given piped water from clean water sources, and toilets connected to sewers to take dirty water away. Sewage treatment plants were built to clean all the dirty water flowing from the cities.

TYPHOID MARY
(c. 1870–1938)

Typhoid Mary, whose real name was Mary Mallon, was at the centre of several **epidemics** of typhoid in New York City, USA. In 1904, there was an outbreak of typhoid in an area of New York where Mary worked as a cook. It was discovered that Mary had the typhoid bacteria in her body, but did not suffer from the disease. The disease had spread in the food she handled. In 1907, she was put in an isolation centre to stop her giving the disease to anyone else. She was released after promising not to work as a cook again. In 1914, another outbreak was traced back to her, and she was put in isolation for the rest of her life. In all, she infected 53 people – three of them died.

Health care for all

At the beginning of the 20th century, many people who were poor and ill had no means of getting treatment. A trip to the doctor or a hospital was an expense most could not afford. Government health care for the poor began in the early decades of the 20th century. The first people to be helped were mothers, babies, and young children. However, everyone else still had to pay up or suffer. Then the idea of health insurance was born. In the United Kingdom, the National Insurance Act of 1911 meant that workers who paid a small amount of "national insurance" from their wages each week could see a doctor when they needed. In the United States, private health insurance companies were set up – for those who could afford it.

Modern health care is available in developing countries. This patient in Tanzania, Africa is being examined with a portable **ultrasound** machine.

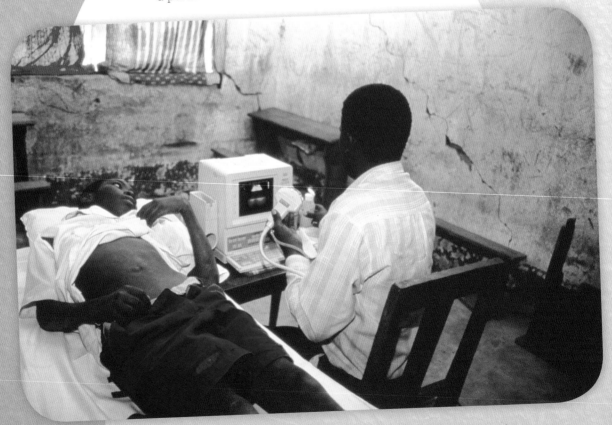

The National Health Service

In 1948, the UK government introduced free health care for all – rich and poor. It set up the National Health Service (NHS). The NHS offers access to family doctors, dentists, hospitals, ambulances, and many other services. The service is paid for by general taxation and so is mostly free at the point of use. The NHS is the largest organization of any kind in Europe, and is extremely costly to run. Only a very few countries have this sort of system.

Today, it is common to see both male and female doctors on a ward round.

WOMEN IN MODERN MEDICINE

In 1900, practically all doctors were men. There were only a handful of women doctors. In the world of medicine, women were seen as carers, as they were at home. The situation began to change during World War I. There were two factors. First, men were needed for fighting the war, and second, more doctors were needed to treat the thousands of wounded soldiers returning from the trenches. So women trained as doctors. The number of women doctors has slowly increased since. In some developed countries, such as the United Kingdom, nearly half of doctors are women. At the same time, almost all nurses are still female.

Diet and fitness

You probably know that what you eat is very important for your health. Food gives your body all the things it needs to grow, to work, and to repair itself. In 1900, people knew that eating certain foods helped to stop them getting certain diseases, but they did not know why. The mystery was solved by British chemist Frederick Hopkins. He discovered that chemicals called amino acids are needed to stay healthy, and that if you do not get enough of them in your food, you get ill. We now call these chemicals vitamins.

Today, we recognize that doing exercise helps to keep you healthy. Exercise makes your heart muscles work harder, and so keeps them strong. Exercise also uses up the energy in some of the food you eat. This stops you putting on too much weight, which would be bad for your heart.

FITNESS TODAY

These days we eat more fatty foods, such as cakes, biscuits, and crisps, than people did 100 years ago. People also do less physical jobs. This means that doing exercise is very important in order to stay fit and healthy.

The girl on the right is suffering from rickets, a condition where bones are softened by a lack of vitamin D in the diet. This condition was common across the world until the early years of the 20th century, and remains a problem in many developing countries today.

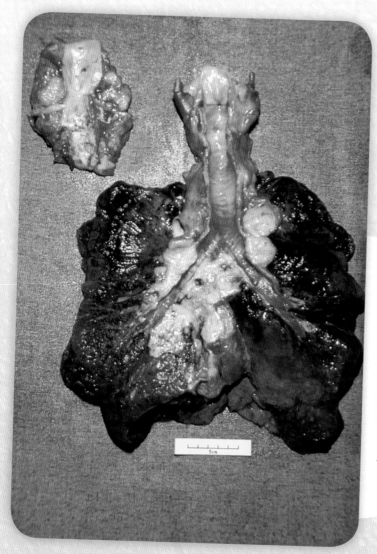

This is a set of lungs taken from a patient who had lung cancer. Healthy lungs are pale and full.

COMMON CONFUSIONS

Cause and effect

People often argue about the causes of disease. For example, some people might say that it is safe to smoke. It is okay, they say, because they know people who have smoked all their lives and do not have lung cancer. Even so, they are mistaken. Some people who have never smoked get lung cancer, and some people who have always smoked do not. That is because several factors affect your chances of getting a disease. The fact is that if you do smoke, your chances of getting cancer are much greater.

Health campaigns

Even though we know that a healthy diet and exercise are good for us, many people in developed countries are overweight or obese (seriously overweight). This problem is getting worse – it is known as the obesity epidemic. Many people also smoke, which we know increases the risk of getting cancer and other diseases. That is why governments introduce health campaigns to try to educate people. In the United Kingdom, the government has run a "five-a-day" campaign, meaning you should eat five portions of fruit or vegetables each day to stay healthy.

The effects of war

The two world wars were a huge factor in the progress of medicine and health in the 20th century. The main reason for the changes was the need to treat injured service personnel such as soldiers, sailors, and airmen.

Injuries in World War I

New types of weapons were used for the first time during World War I. They included high-explosive shells that produced flying lumps of metal, poison gas, and heavy machine guns. More soldiers were killed and wounded than in any previous war. Because injuries were so bad, surgeons had to try new techniques. One important technique they developed was the use of skin grafts for burns and other injuries. In a skin graft, surgeons replace damaged skin on part of the body with skin from another part of the body. Surgeons also made advances in brain surgery to treat head wounds, which were very common. After the war ended, surgical techniques were far better than they were when it started.

A soldier wounded in battle during World War I waits on a stretcher to receive treatment.

These US Army medics are performing a blood transfusion on a beach during World War II.

Blood transfusions

In a transfusion, a patient's lost blood is replaced by blood from another person (called a donor). Before 1900, many patients died during operations because they lost too much blood. Surgeons tried transfusions, but patients still died. The mystery was solved by Austrian scientist Karl Landsteiner. In 1901, he discovered that mixing blood from two different patients made the blood clot. He found that there are four different types of blood, which he called O, A, B, and AB. A blood transfusion works only when a patient's blood is replaced with blood of the same type. Blood transfusions saved the lives of thousands of soldiers in both world wars.

ERNST CHAIN
(1906–1979)
AND HOWARD FLOREY
(1898–1968)

Ernst Chain and Howard Florey were the scientists who first gave penicillin to a human patient. A few days after World War II began, the British government made money available for research into penicillin. Chain and Florey, working at Oxford University, got some of the money. They read articles by Alexander Fleming and set to work. It took a long time to grow enough penicillin for their test. After successful tests on mice, they finally gave the drug to a human patient in 1941. The patient, suffering from a terrible infection, quickly improved, but later died after the penicillin ran out.

The story of penicillin

In 1928, Scottish scientist Alexander Fleming had an amazingly lucky accident. Returning to his laboratory after a holiday, he found that a piece of **fungus** had fallen into a dish containing some bacteria. The bacteria around the fungus had died. Fleming identified the fungus as *Penicillium*.

Fleming found that *Penicillium* contains a chemical that kills bacteria. He called the chemical penicillin. He realized that penicillin could be used to fight infections caused by bacteria. He had made the first antibiotic. Fleming could not find a way of making penicillin in large amounts. When World War II began, scientists realized that the drug would save lives. They found a way to produce it on a large scale.

By 1944, this penicillin factory was sending 15,000 doses a day to sick soldiers.

WORD STATION
fungus organism that feeds and grows on organic matter, such as moulds, mushrooms, and toadstools

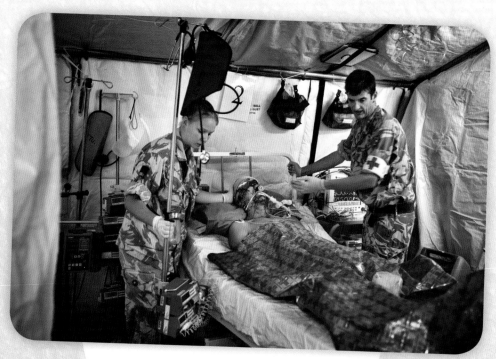

A modern-day field hospital contains state-of-the-art medical equipment.

COMMON CONFUSIONS

Plastic surgery and cosmetic surgery

Plastic surgery reconstructs parts of a patient's body, usually after they have suffered an injury through a serious accident. Plastic surgery began during World War II, when surgeons began to repair the injured or burned faces of soldiers, sailors, and airmen. Cosmetic surgery is the use of plastic surgery to improve a person's appearance. Many people choose to have cosmetic surgery because it gives them more confidence in their appearance.

By 1944, penicillin was being used on the battlefield. It saved the lives of thousands of Allied soldiers. Penicillin is still a popular antibiotic today.

Wounded at home

Soldiers, sailors, and airmen were not the only casualties of World War II. In the United Kingdom and other countries, health services had to treat people caught in bombing raids on towns and cities. Health services had to quickly grow and improve to deal with the number of casualties. In the United Kingdom, this growth was one factor in the formation of the National Health Service (see page 23) soon after the war. People also thought that people who had suffered in the war should have access to healthcare.

Global health care

Health care is different in every country. Around the world, governments, international organizations (such as the United Nations), charities, and volunteers all have roles in health care. Despite modern drugs and other treatments, some diseases kill millions of people across the globe.

Health in developed countries

In most developed countries, there is a mixture of government health care and private health care. People can see a doctor, get emergency medical treatment, and have operations when they need to. Sometimes the treatment is paid for by the government. Sometimes people pay a private health insurance company, which pays for the treatment. In these countries, public health is mostly of a high standard. Most housing is of good quality, and most people have access to clean water and good **sanitation**.

LIFE EXPECTANCY AND SPENDING

There is a strong link between how much a country spends on health care and how long its citizens can expect to live. Generally, in countries that spend less money, **life expectancy** is shorter. It can be lower than 45 years in very poor countries, such as Afghanistan. In countries that spend more money, life expectancy is longer. However, some countries are exceptions. Cuba spends just US$200 per person each year, but life expectancy is 77 years for men and 80 for women. One factor is that the Cuban health care system educates people to prevent disease. Most Western countries spend more than ten times as much for each person.

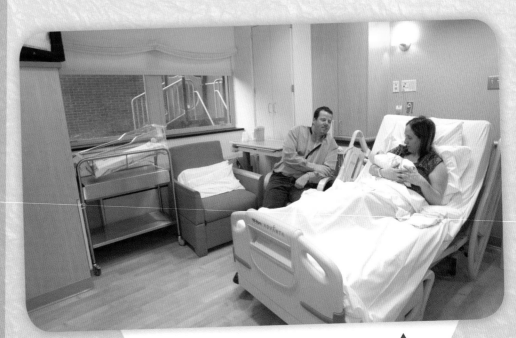

Most patients in developed countries can expect the best medical care in clean, comfortable hospitals.

Health in developing countries

Many economically developing countries cannot afford to run government health care programmes. Most people are poor and have no access to health care. The sick are helped in their communities or by overseas charities. For most, there is no chance of life-saving surgery for illnesses such as heart failure. Public health is not good, either. In cities, millions live in slums, with no fresh water or sanitation.

Diseases such as cholera and typhoid can spread easily in these conditions, and millions of children die each year from simple problems such as diarrhoea. Many people cannot afford to buy healthy food, and suffer from diseases caused by a lack of vitamins.

These shanty houses in the Philippines are right next to a filthy river.

Generally, health care is better in economically developed countries than it is in economically developing countries. However, the poor in some *developed* countries, such as the United States, have less access to health care, and the rich in *developing* countries can pay for the latest modern treatments.

Killer diseases

We can now be treated successfully for many diseases that would have killed people 100 years ago. Some diseases have been almost completely beaten by worldwide vaccination and education programmes. They include smallpox, polio, measles, mumps, and tetanus. However, some diseases are still killers because so far we have no drugs or **vaccines** for them.

Malaria is a disease caused by a tiny parasite in the blood, spread by mosquitoes. It causes fever, headache, and diarrhoea, and often kills. Malaria mostly affects people in tropical countries. In 2008, 243 million people around the world caught malaria, mostly in Africa, and mostly children. A million of them died. On average, malaria kills a child every 30 seconds. Anti-malaria drugs help to stop people catching malaria, and so can mosquito nets over beds. The mosquitoes that carry the disease can be killed by insecticides. But malaria continues to kill.

This child's mother and grandmother can only wait and hope as he is treated for malaria.

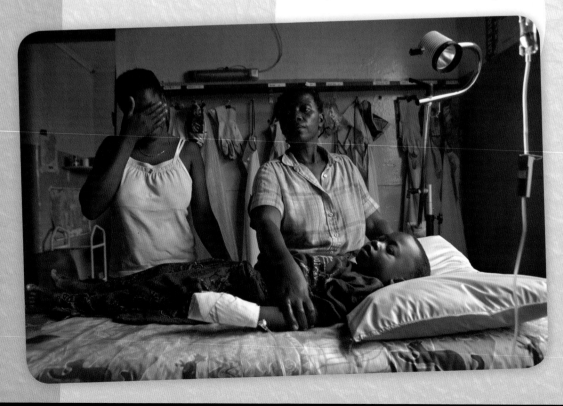

WORD STATION
vaccine substance given to a patient that makes his or her immune system ready to fight a particular disease

Flu epidemics have killed millions of people in the past. Here, masked volunteers hand out food to infected children in 1917.

HIV/AIDS

HIV is a type of **virus** spread by infected blood and sexual contact. It attacks the body's **immune system**, which defends the body against infections. People infected with HIV eventually become ill because of infections. This disease is called AIDS (acquired immune deficiency syndrome). Eventually, they die. In 2008, 33 million were suffering from HIV/AIDS and 70 per cent of them lived in Africa. Another 3 million caught it during the year. So far, HIV/AIDS had killed 27 million people.

At the moment, there is no cure or vaccine for HIV/AIDS. Even so, the spread of the virus can be contained through good education, with free condoms being available in many countries. Sufferers can live longer by taking drugs that slow the speed at which the virus reproduces itself. However, the drugs are too expensive for most people, and only 5 million people have access to them.

COMMON CONFUSIONS

Flu vaccines

For most people, getting flu means a few days in bed. However, flu can be deadly, especially for young children and old people. An outbreak of flu can spread across the globe, killing thousands of people. Many people think that getting a flu vaccine stops you getting flu. But vaccines can only prevent one sort of flu. If another sort comes along, you can catch it. Some people also think that taking antibiotics can get rid of a cold or flu. Antibiotics cannot do this because they fight infections caused by bacteria, and colds and flu are caused by viruses.

The World Health Organization

The **World Health Organization** (WHO) is part of the United Nations. WHO is made up of 193 member countries. WHO works to improve the health of people all over the globe. This means there is a global approach to health problems, instead of countries working by themselves. WHO has more than 8,000 experts working for it.

WHO does many different jobs. It works on the fight against killer diseases, such as HIV/AIDS, tuberculosis, and malaria. It tracks **epidemics** of diseases such as flu, and helps to plan how to stop them spreading. It organizes worldwide vaccination programmes against diseases such as polio. Teams of experts from WHO are ready to help when there are outbreaks of disease after natural disasters or during wars. WHO also keeps track of how many people are suffering from different diseases around the world. This data helps countries to plan their health care for the future.

WHO's most important work is in developing countries. It helps to improve the health of poor people whose governments cannot provide them with health care.

Red Cross workers are unloading food and medical supplies for Kenyans made homeless by a political crisis in 2008.

The Smile Train charity carries out surgery on children with cleft palates.

Charities

Charities have an important role in modern medicine. Some charities focus their work on a particular disease. For example, there are charities that raise money to help people suffering from HIV/AIDS, and charities that raise money for research into the causes of cancer. Some charities raise money to send medical teams to treat poor people in developing countries, or people caught up in natural disasters or wars. Charities can be international, national, or local organizations. Local organizations may help their local hospital, for example, to raise money for a new piece of medical equipment.

Traditional and alternative medicine

For thousands of years, people have used plants to treat infections, diseases, and symptoms such as pain and fever. These traditional medicines were discovered over time, probably by accident. In the last few decades, similar sorts of treatments, that do not rely on modern drugs or high-tech equipment, have become popular in the West. These treatments are known as alternative medicine.

Traditional medicines

Traditional medicines (also known as indigenous medicines) are still used by millions of people around the world. This is often where modern medicines are not available, or are too expensive. Sometimes people do not trust modern medicine, but would rather use medicines that their parents used. In some countries, 80 per cent of people rely on traditional medicine. Some traditional medicines are also used as alternative medicines in the West.

Many modern medicines are substances that come from plants, or are copies of substances from plants. An example is the painkiller aspirin, which originally came from a plant called white willow. This plant had been used for centuries to treat pain and fever.

MEDICINES FROM PLANTS

Here are some examples of modern drugs that were originally found in plants.

- *Aspirin* a form of salicin, which was found in willow bark. For relief of pain and fever.
- *Quinine* found in the bark of the cinchona tree. For prevention and treatment of malaria.
- *Digitalis* found in the foxglove. For the treatment of heart conditions.

Here you can see all sorts of traditional medicines for sale on a market stall in China.

▶

This rhinoceros has been killed by a poacher for its horns. Some people believe rhino horns have medicinal properties.

Is natural safe?

Many people think that because traditional herbal medicines are natural, they must be safe to use. This is not always true. Some herbal medicines can be harmful to some people, perhaps because of an allergic reaction. They can also interfere with modern drugs if the two are taken together.

Controversial medicines

Some traditional medicines are controversial today. For example, some use ingredients from endangered animals in their preparation, including the tiger, sea horse, and rhinoceros.

Rhinoceros horn is used in many countries, including China, India, and Malaysia. The horn is ground up and mixed with boiling water to make a medicine that people believe will cure all sorts of complaints, from fever to snakebites. So many rhinoceroses have been illegally hunted for their horns that their numbers have dramatically declined. There is no scientific evidence that this medicine works, and campaigners around the world are trying to convince people not to buy products containing rhino horn.

Alternative medicine

In Western countries, many people use "alternative" or complementary medical treatments, such as homeopathy or acupuncture. These treatments do not use modern drugs or surgical techniques. Some treatments that are thought of in the West as alternative treatments actually just come from other countries, where they are everyday treatments that have been popular for centuries. Yoga is an example. It originated in India more than 6,000 years ago. Although most Western people practice yoga as a form of relaxation, some do believe it prevents some illnesses. Other alternative treatments have been developed in the last few decades.

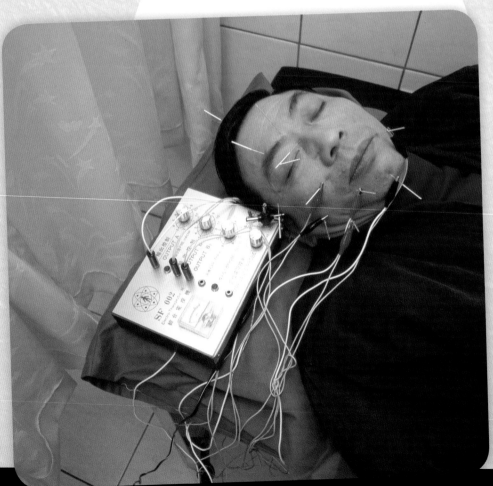

Acupuncture involves pushing very thin needles into specific locations on the body.

THE PLACEBO EFFECT

Doctors and scientists think that many alternative therapies work for some patients because the patients think they will work. A therapy works because the patient believes in it, and not because it has any physical effect. This is known as the **placebo effect**. Placebo medicines, which contain no drugs at all, are often used in clinical trials.

Many people think that yoga and meditation can help prevent disease.

At first, doctors and other medical professionals were suspicious and sceptical about all alternative medicine. This was because alternative medicines are not backed up by scientific evidence or **clinical trials**. Also, the therapists who practised them did not have medical qualifications. More recently, some doctors have accepted that some treatments, such as acupuncture, work for some patients. Some alternative treatments are now paid for by health services.

Popular alternative medicines

- *Homeopathy* is based on the idea that if taking large amounts of a chemical gives a person the symptoms of a disease, taking a tiny amount of the same chemical will cure the disease. Homeopathy was founded by German doctor Samuel Hahnemann (1755–1843). There is no scientific evidence that it works.

- *Chiropractic* was founded by an American called Daniel David Palmer (1845–1913). Chiropractors believe that some illnesses and diseases are caused by bones pressing against nerves in the spinal column. They bend and twist the spine to try to cure problems. There is evidence that some patients benefit from this treatment.

- *Reflexology* is based on the idea that massaging the feet in certain places can help cure various medical conditions. It was developed in the 1930s by Eunice Ingham. There seems to be little scientific evidence that this treatment is effective for any medical condition.

Where are we now?

Medicine has come a long way since the early 20th century. Thanks to discoveries and research, our knowledge about how the human body works and how diseases affect it has greatly improved. We have new drugs, such as antibiotics, to fight disease. Complex operations that were out of the question a century ago, such as eye surgery and organ transplants, are routine today. A person who falls ill today has a far better chance of surviving than a person who fell ill in 1900. Public health has improved, so people are less likely to catch diseases in the first place.

It is not all good news, however. Despite all these advances, there are still diseases that we do not know how to treat, or even if we will ever be able to, such as cancer and HIV/AIDS.

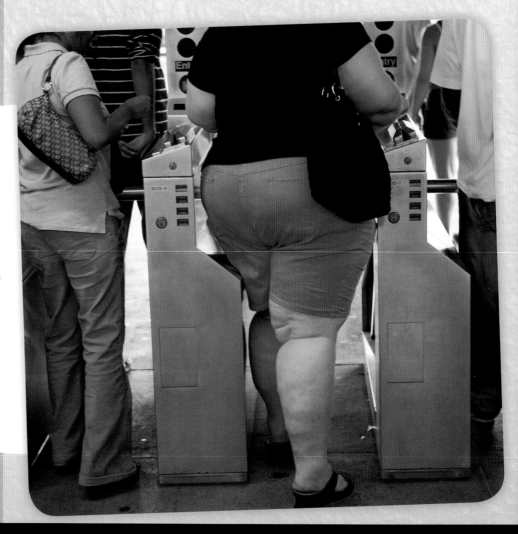

Obesity is a new health problem facing many people today. It is common in Western countries.

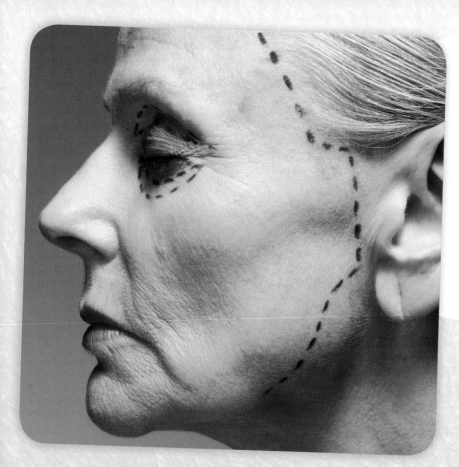

Medicine is increasingly being used to alter a person's appearance.

On the horizon

Researchers are studying cells called **stem cells**. These can grow into any sort of cell, such as nerve cells, blood cells, and skin cells. Stem cells could be used to regrow or repair parts of the body. For example, growing brain cells from stem cells may help sufferers of **Alzheimer's disease**. However, the use of stem cells is controversial. Some stem cells used for experimental treatments are gathered from human **embryos**, which some people think is wrong.

The future

If the pace of change continues as it has over the last hundred years, it is hard to imagine what the world of medicine will be like at the end of the 21st century. What discoveries might we make about the human body? Will we overcome current problems such as dementia and cancer? New diseases may appear to challenge us – especially as increasing global travel and the effects of climate change mean that diseases once limited to one part of the world find new places to thrive. Perhaps the best change of all would be equal access to health care for everybody on the planet.

NEW PROBLEMS

A new factor for change is the increasing lifespan of people in developed countries. Better medicine has allowed people to live longer, but with old age comes new problems. Many people who live into their 80s and 90s suffer from failing joints and dementia (impaired brain function that causes memory loss and personality changes). Medicine has to respond to these new challenges.

WORD STATION
embryo unborn baby, before the stage when its organs have developed (normally before it is eight weeks old)

Timeline

1901	Austrian scientist Karl Landsteiner discovers that there are several different types of blood (later called blood groups)
1910	German scientist Paul Ehrlich develops the first **synthetic** drug, called salvarsan
1911	The National Insurance Act comes into force in the United Kingdom
1914–1918	World War I
1918	A flu pandemic kills between 50 and 100 million people worldwide
1927	The first **vaccines** for the diseases tuberculosis and tetanus are developed
1928	Scottish scientist Alexander Fleming discovers penicillin, the first antibiotic
1938	Typhoid Mary, who was the source of several typhoid outbreaks, dies aged 68
1939–1945	World War II
1940s	The **ultrasound** scanner is developed
1944	Penicillin saves the lives of thousands of soldiers fighting in World War II
1945	The first vaccine for flu is developed
1948	The National Health Service is set up in the United Kingdom
1948	The **World Health Organization** (WHO) is formed
1950s	British physicist Harold Hopkins invents the fibroscope, a flexible **endoscope**

1953	Francis Crick and James Watson discover the structure of **DNA.** US surgeon John Gibbon uses a heart-lung bypass machine during surgery for the first time.
1955	A vaccination against polio, developed by US doctor Jonas Salk, comes into use
1957	The drug thalidomide is given to patients for the first time
1960s	The government health services Medicare and Medicaid are set up in the United States. The portable heart defibrillator is developed. The checking of babies before birth using ultrasound scanners begins.
1964	US surgeon Charles Dotter invents angioplasty for clearing blocked **coronary arteries**
1967	South African surgeon Christiaan Barnard performs the first heart transplant operation
1969	US surgeon Harry Buncke performs the first operation to use **microsurgery**
1970s	The computed tomography (CT) scanner is developed. The magnetic resonance imaging (MRI) scanner is developed.
1978	Louise Brown, the first "test tube" baby, is born in England
1980	The disease smallpox is believed to have been eradicated
1983	HIV, the disease that causes AIDS, is identified
1990s	The first laser eye surgeries are performed
1996	Dolly the sheep, the first mammal to be cloned, is born
2003	The Human Genome Project is completed
2008	More than 33 million people around the world suffer from HIV/AIDS

Glossary

Alzheimer's disease form of mental deterioration that can occur in middle or old age, resulting in memory loss, personality changes, and impaired judgement

anaesthetic substance used in operations to stop a patient feeling pain

clinical trial series of experiments designed to test how well a new drug or new medical technique works, and whether it is safe for patients

cornea transparent layer at the front of a person's eye, which can become opaque (not able to be seen through) because of certain illnesses

coronary artery large blood vessel that carries oxygenated blood to the heart muscles

cystic fibrosis disease that is inherited by children from their parents. It can cause the lungs to become clogged with thick mucus.

diagnose identify the nature of a disease or injury through examination

DNA short for deoxyribonucleic acid, the complex chemical that holds the information contained in a person's genes

embryo unborn baby, before the stage when its organs have developed (normally before it is eight weeks old)

endoscope medical instrument that can be inserted into the body and allows doctors to see inside their patients

epidemic rapid spread of a disease through an area of population

fungus organism that feeds and grows on organic matter, such as moulds, mushrooms, and toadstools

gene piece of information stored in cells that passes hereditary information from parent to child

immune system system that fights infection in a person's body

keyhole surgery surgery that is carried out through a very small cut in the body

life expectancy measure of the average age that either men or women live to in a country or region, given in years

microsurgery surgery carried out on very tiny structures in the body, with the aid of specialized instruments

neonatal to do with newborn children

pharmaceutical to do with medicines, their use, and manufacture

placebo effect benefit from a treatment that occurs because the patient believes in it

psychotherapy treatment of mental problems using psychological methods

sanitation systems that bring fresh water to people, and take away and clean sewage

sickle-cell disease disease in which red blood cells are distorted, so that they cannot carry oxygen efficiently

stem cell cell that can change into any sort of cell in a human body, such as a blood cell, nerve cell, or skin cell

synthetic artificial

syphilis sexually transmitted disease that can infect the skin, bones, muscles, and brain

ultrasound sound of extremely high frequency (too high for humans to hear). Ultrasound is used to look at babies inside the mother's womb.

vaccine substance given to a patient that makes his or her immune system ready to fight a particular disease

virus tiny particle that invades cells and multiplies in them

World Health Organization (WHO) body within the United Nations that works to improve global health through research and technical support

X-ray type of radiation that passes through soft tissue but not bone and is used to see structures inside the body. It is also the name of an image taken with X-rays.

Find out more

Books

Ethical Debates in Modern Medicine (Dilemmas in Modern Science), Ray Lovegrove (Evans Brothers, 2008)

From Fail to Win! Learning from Bad Ideas: Medicine, Rebecca Vickers (Raintree, 2011)

Introduction to Genes and DNA, Anna Claybourne (Usborne Publishing, 2006)

Medical Technology (Sci-Hi: Science and Technology), Ann Fullick (Raintree, 2011)

What are the Limits of Organ Transplantation? (Sci-Hi: Science Issues), Anna Clayborne (Raintree, 2012)

What is the Controversy Over Stem Cell Research? (Sci-Hi: Science Issues), Isobel Thomas (Raintree, 2012)

Websites

www.channel4.com/explore/surgerylive/history.html
Discover more about the history of surgery on this website.

www.sciencemuseum.org.uk/broughttolife
The history of medicine is revealed on the Science Museum's website.

www.who.int
Visit the official website of the World Health Organization to find out about the work they do and some facts about contemporary health issues.

www.bbc.co.uk/schools/gcsebitesize/history/shp/modern
This BBC website contains a useful summary of developments in modern medicine.

More topics to research

Try researching further into some of the topics that you have read about in this book. Is there any particular theme that you are interested in? Here are some ideas to get you started:

- The roles of William Beverage and Aneurin Bevan in the formation of the United Kingdom's National Health Service

- The history of the United States' Medicare and Medicaid services

- The effect of air pollution from burning fuels on people's health, especially in cities

- The spread of malaria, and what effect climate change is having on this

- Finding a clean water supply in developing countries, and the role of charities such as WaterAid

- The effect of shell shock on the soldiers of World War I

- The work of the World Health Organization

- Look at graphs of how life expectancy and infant mortality have changed since 1900

- Robots in the operating theatre

- The rise of modern diseases, such as diabetes

- The ethical debate over the use of embryonic stem cells

- The cover of this book shows a detail from the painting *Operation* by Christian Schad. What does it tell you about medicine in the modern age? The surgeons are wearing gloves and using metal instruments. Do you think this might have been different in the past? If so, how?

Index